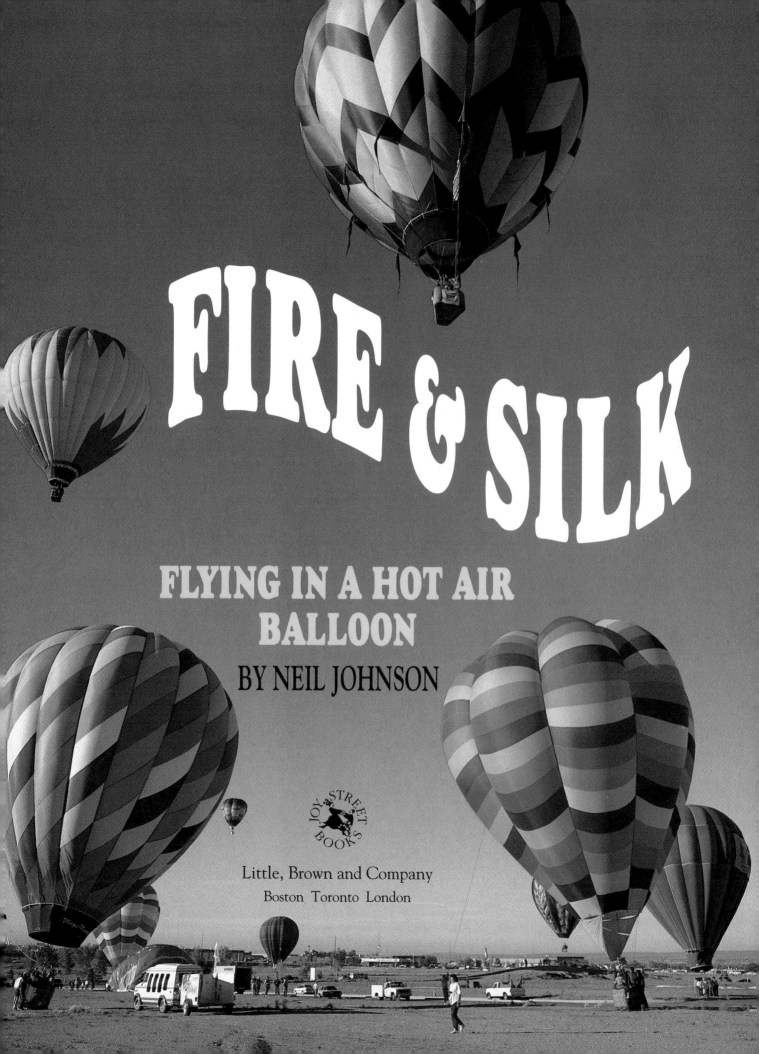

FIRE & SILK

FLYING IN A HOT AIR
BALLOON

BY NEIL JOHNSON

JOY STREET BOOKS

Little, Brown and Company
Boston Toronto London

To my father,
a man whose spirit lifts us all

Many, many thanks to Rex Jennings, the proud pilot of the
beautiful balloon "Jenn Air," and to his wonderful crew,
Lorraine, Jennifer, Janna, Jared, and Jessica.

You have flown so high and so well
That God has joined you in your laughter.

Copyright © 1991 by Neil Johnson

First Edition

Library of Congress Cataloging-in-Publication Data

Johnson, Neil, 1954–
    Fire and silk: flying in a hot air balloon / Neil Johnson. — 1st ed.
      p.   cm.
    Summary: Depicts what it is like to ride in a hot air balloon and
discusses how hot air balloons were invented and how they work.
    ISBN 0-316-46959-9
    1. Ballooning — Pictorial works — Juvenile literature. 2. Hot air
balloons — Pictorial works — Juvenile literature. [1. Hot air
balloons. 2. Ballooning.] I. Title.
GV762.J64   1991
797.5'1'0222 — dc20   90-43215

Joy Street Books are published by
Little, Brown and Company (Inc.)

10 9 8 7 6 5 4 3 2 1

SC

Published simultaneously in Canada
by Little, Brown & Company (Canada) Limited

Printed in Hong Kong

Throughout history, people have looked up at the sky and dreamed about flying. In 1782, two French brothers, Joseph and Etienne Montgolfier, were the first to capture that dream. As an experiment, they lit a fire under the opening of an upside-down paper bag and tied the bag closed to trap the heated air inside. When they let go of the bag, it floated up toward the ceiling!

When air is heated, it becomes lighter, producing lift, the force needed to raise something. Because the heated air inside the Montgolfiers' paper bag was lighter than the air in the room, the bag was lifted up.

The excited brothers immediately began making bigger, stronger bags from silken fabric and paper. Maybe larger balloons would be able to carry passengers! they thought. Because they weren't sure whether it would be safe for humans so high in the sky, they decided to send up a sheep, a duck, and a rooster as the first passengers. In September 1783, the king of France and a large crowd gathered to witness the animals' flight. The balloon soared along for eight minutes and landed two miles away, its passengers safe.

The Montgolfiers then made a giant bag of blue fabric with gold designs and hung a large basket under it. In November 1783, they took this special balloon to Paris. After the Montgolfiers lit a smoky fire under the bag, a scientist and a soldier climbed into the basket, and up they went. They were the first people ever to fly!

Since that first flight, people have learned that balloons, filled with either hot air or gas, could be used for many things: lookouts during war, weather prediction, and long-distance travel. Today, though, people fly modern hot air balloons for fun and sport. There are thousands of registered balloonists in America alone. A new balloon costs about as much as a sports car. Balloons are inexpensive to maintain and run, can be carried to just about anywhere, and can be set up, inflated, and launched in about fifteen minutes.

But hot air balloons cannot be flown at just any time. The pilot, or the person in charge of flying the balloon, must first study the weather to be sure that there is not too much wind and that no storms are coming. The best times to fly are at sunrise or just before sunset, because the wind is usually calmest then.

In the middle of a wide open space, such as a large parking lot or field, the crew members, or the people who help the pilot, unload the basket and the balloon. Balloonists call the balloon the envelope. Most early envelopes were made from silk, but modern ones are made from more airtight and less expensive cloth such as nylon. Baskets are usually made of wicker because it is strong and light and flexible enough to absorb the impact of rough landings.

The crew attaches the envelope to the basket with strong cables, then stretches it out along the ground. When it is lying out flat, the envelope is almost a hundred feet long.

The balloon is now ready to be inflated.

First, an inflation fan, which sounds like a lawn mower, blows cold air into the balloon until it is about three-quarters inflated. While the balloon is expanding, a crew member holds the crown line, which is attached to the top of the balloon, to keep the balloon steady in case of wind gusts.

In less than five minutes, the folds of colorful, silky cloth grow and take on the shape of a giant teardrop. At this point the pilot walks around the balloon checking for any holes in the cloth or seams. Normally, the envelope should not be walked on. But sometimes, passengers or crew members take their shoes off and carefully walk inside the balloon while it is being inflated by the fan.

Once the balloon is three-quarters in-flated, the pilot turns on the burner, which is fueled by tanks of propane strapped inside the basket. When the pilot squeezes the blast valve on the burner, the propane comes rushing out and is lit by a tiny flame, called a pilot light. Suddenly a flame almost eight feet long shoots out with a *roar!* This flame heats the air inside the balloon.

The pilot uses the burner until the air in the balloon is hot enough—and light enough—to lift the envelope off the ground. The person holding the crown line makes sure the balloon doesn't stand up too fast and begin swinging back and forth. In just a couple of minutes, the balloon has become fully inflated, and the air inside it is getting hot enough to be almost ready for lift-off. The balloon rises up and towers over the basket—as tall as a seven-story building!

While the crew holds on to the basket, the pilot and passengers climb in. Most balloon baskets hold up to three people. Then the pilot turns on the burner again. This blast of the burner will make the air in the balloon hot enough to lift the weight of the basket and its passengers. The pilot, the passengers, and even the crew on the ground feel a wonderful moment of anticipation as the balloon quickly becomes lighter and lighter. It is time to fly!

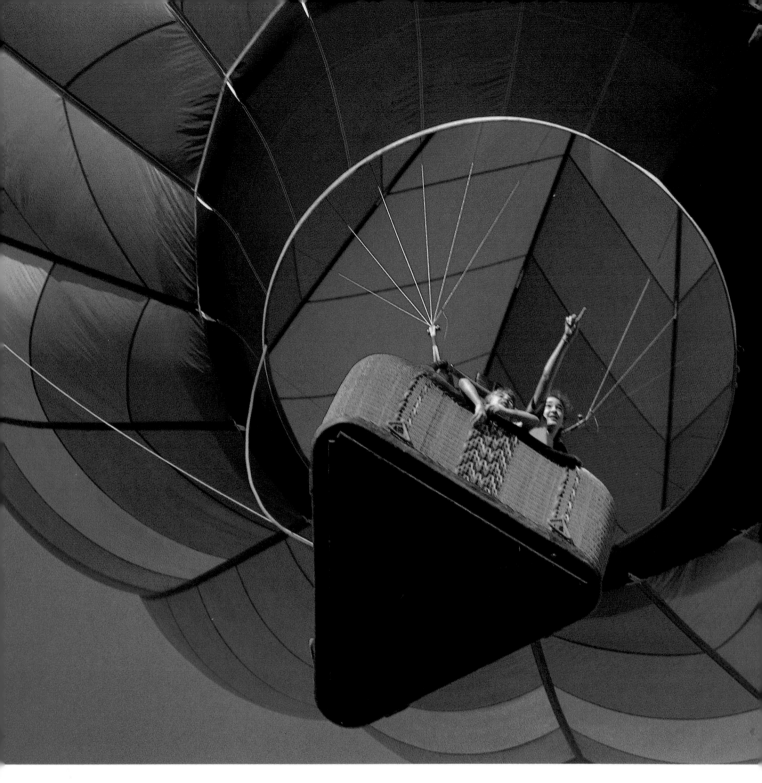

Gently, the balloon leaves the ground. Lift-off feels smooth and steady, as if a friendly giant had picked up the basket and tenderly begun raising it to the sky.

In an airborne balloon, passengers can't feel or hear the wind because they are flying right along with it. The balloon's speed is exactly the same as the wind's speed. As a result, flying in a balloon is quiet and peaceful. The silence is broken only occasionally when the pilot lets out a blast from the burner to keep the air inside the balloon hot.

The thought of flying in a balloon is scary to many people because the balloon soars so high and the basket seems so small and open. They may be afraid they will fall out or the cables holding the basket will break. But once in the air, passengers usually discover that the basket feels surprisingly solid and safe. The cables are strong, the wicker is sturdy, and the basket's tall sides give a protected feeling.

How high the balloon flies, or its altitude, depends on how hot the air in the balloon is. To fly at a steady altitude, the pilot turns on the burner for a few seconds every few minutes. If the pilot uses the burner more, the balloon will slowly go higher. If he or she uses the burner less or not at all, the air in the balloon will begin to cool, and the balloon will slowly go down.

Most hot air balloons can fly for about one or two hours before the fuel for the burner begins to run low. If the burner were to stop working or if the fuel were to run out, the balloon would cool and go down, but it would not drop quickly enough to cause serious damage. The large, inflated balloon would act like a parachute and carry its passengers safely to the ground.

A balloon cannot be steered in the same way that a car, an airplane, or a boat can be. Balloons fly wherever the wind takes them. At different altitudes, however, the wind sometimes blows in different directions. So by varying the balloon's altitude, the pilot can control which direction the balloon is heading.

But the only way to know the direction of the wind at various altitudes is to experiment, going up and down and seeing which way the balloon goes. Navigating, or trying to steer the balloon in these various winds, is the hardest part of

ballooning. Pilots usually have a general idea where their balloon is going, but because of the different winds, they never know exactly where they will end up.

Nor can pilots be sure how long it will take to travel a certain distance. How fast the balloon goes depends on how fast the wind is blowing. Depending on the wind, an hour's balloon flight may cover one, ten, or twenty miles.

The challenge and unpredictability of riding the winds are part of what makes hot air ballooning such an adventure.

While the balloon is flying, the crew follows it in the chase vehicle, ready to help the pilot and pick up the balloon when it lands. The balloon flies with the wind, but the chase vehicle must drive back and forth on different roads to stay close to it. Chase crews are constantly looking up to track the balloon, then

looking down at their road maps to decide the best route to take to follow the balloon. Crews also stay in close touch with the pilot by two-way radio. So if there are many trees and the crew loses sight of the balloon, the pilot radios the chase crew about the balloon's position and which roads to take.

No two balloon flights are ever the same. A balloon can soar as high as ten thousand feet—almost two miles straight up—or, for fun, it can dip down and touch the tops of tall trees or even the surface of a pond or lake for a second or two.

The view from a balloon is better than from any other flying machine. The open basket allows a clear view in every direction. Trees, roads, and homes look completely different from the air. Wide highways look like long, thin lines twisting off into the distance. Tall buildings look stubby and short. Often, dogs will

see the balloon and chase it, barking excitedly. Sometimes, cows or horses will be startled by the loud noise of the balloon's burner in the sky and scurry away across their fields. People going about their business on the ground will almost always stop what they are doing to watch a balloon pass over.

Although it is fun to fly over a city and look down on its skyscrapers, neighborhoods, and curious people, most pilots are more comfortable flying over open countryside where it is much easier to find safe places to land.

Since balloons cannot turn around and land in the field where they took off, the pilot must look ahead to find another open field. Once the pilot spots a field in the flight path, he or she begins allowing the air to cool so that the balloon can gently drop down.

Landing in a small area is difficult. The pilot must time the use of the burner just right, because if the balloon comes down too fast or too slow, it could miss the landing site.

When flying low, approaching the landing site, the pilot must always watch out for electric power lines and trees. Power lines are the biggest danger in ballooning. The thin wires are difficult to see from above and are full of huge amounts of electricity. And while landing in trees is not dangerous for the balloonists, it can be for the balloon. Sharp branches could poke holes in the envelope.

Just before landing or just as the balloon touches the ground, the pilot pulls the vent line to open the vent at the top of the envelope. With the hot air escaping through the opening, the envelope begins to deflate slowly.

If there is not much wind, landing is gentle and easy. But in a heavier wind, landing may be a bit bumpy. Passengers must crouch down low and hold on tightly to the basket. The wind may blow the balloon across the ground, dragging the tipped basket until the balloon deflates enough to stop acting as a sail. If the ground is rocky and uneven, riding the landing out may be rough and bouncy for a few seconds.

With its top vent open and the hot air escaping, the balloon slowly settles onto the ground. When the chase crew arrives, everyone works together to squeeze the remaining air out of the envelope and stuff it back into its canvas bag. Then the packed-up envelope and the basket are loaded onto the chase vehicle.

After the work is done, everyone celebrates. As they exchange highlights of the day's flight and chase and retell earlier balloon adventures, it is as if no one wants the experience to end.

First-time flyers get special attention. Everyone toasts them warmly, and the pilot recites to them the Balloonists' Prayer:

The winds have welcomed you with softness.
The sun has blessed you with his warm hands.
You have flown so high and so well
That God has joined you in your laughter.
And He has set you gently back again
Into the loving arms of Mother Earth.

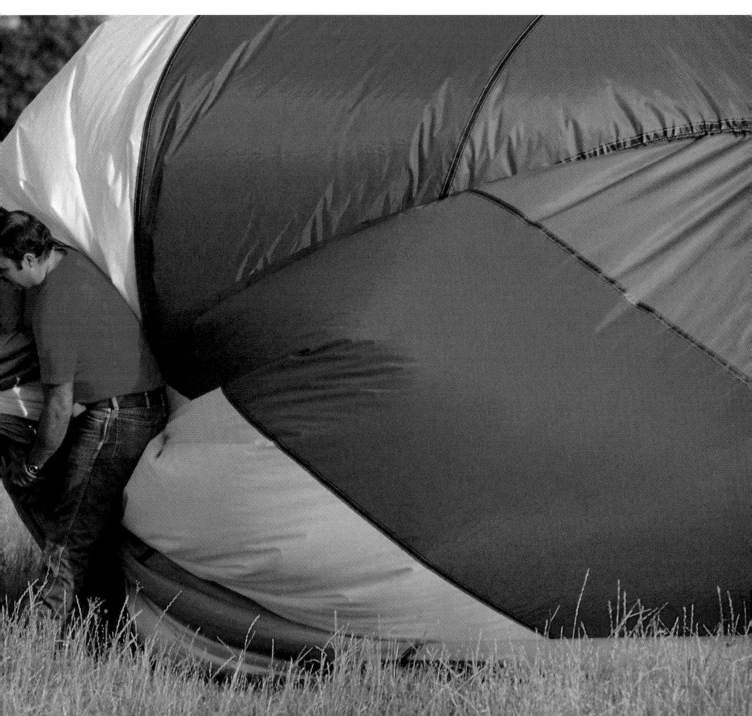

Almost all balloonists love to gather together and fly their hot air balloons as a group. They believe the excitement and adventure of ballooning is best when shared. It's fun to look out from an airborne balloon and see other colorful and majestic balloons flying nearby. And for observers on the ground, the more balloons, the better the spectacle.

Balloon pilots also play games in their balloons. In one game, called "Fox and Hounds," one balloon (the "fox") takes off first and uses different winds to zigzag through the sky. A little later, the other balloons (the "hounds") take off. The hound who lands closest to the fox wins.

In another game, one balloon will fly for a distance, land, and set up a huge "X" on the ground. The rest of the balloons follow and try to drop beanbag "bombs" as near to the center of the "X" as they can.

Imagine what a sky full of hundreds of hot air balloons is like! Just about every part of the country has its own hot air balloon festival. Albuquerque, New Mexico, hosts the largest balloon festival anywhere. Each October, balloonists

go there from around the world to fill the sky each morning and evening with as many as five hundred balloons of every color and design—even special shapes, such as animals and clowns.

Today, there are many ways for people to fly: small airplanes,
big jets, helicopters, and rocket ships. But for people who
are not in a hurry to get anywhere in particular, who
are thrilled by spectacular bird's-eye views, by
the sight of gigantic shapes of brilliant,
silky cloth, and by the peace and
quiet of unmotored flight,
the best way to fly is
the oldest way: in a
hot air balloon.